You're cordially invited to:

Halloween Mysteries

For Midnight Reading:

10 Creepy True Stories

that happened

on HALLOWEEN!

MAX P. MILLS

This document is geared towards providing exact and reliable information in regard to the topic and issue covered. The publication is sold with the idea that the publisher is not required to render accounting, officially permitted, or otherwise, qualified services. If advice is necessary, legal or professional, a practiced individual in the profession should be ordered.

- From a Declaration of Principles which was accepted and approved equally by a Committee of the American Bar Association and a Committee of Publishers and Associations.

with written permission from the publisher. All rights reserved.

The information provided herein is stated to be truthful and consistent, in that any liability, in terms of inattention or otherwise, by any usage or abuse of any policies, processes, or directions contained within is the solitary and utter responsibility of the recipient reader. Under no circumstances will any legal responsibility or blame be held against the publisher for any reparation, damages, or monetary loss due to the information herein, either directly or indirectly.

Respective authors own all copyrights not held by the publisher.

The information herein is offered for informational purposes solely, and is universal as so. The presentation of the information is without contract or any type of guarantee assurance.

The trademarks that are used are without any consent, and the publication of the trademark is without permission or backing by the trademark owner. All trademarks and brands within this book are for clarifying purposes only and are owned by the owners themselves, not affiliated with this document.

INTRODUCTION

For most of us, Halloween is a special time for Autumn fun. It's a time for us to dress up in scary costumes and have some fun around the neighbourhood, scaring the locals!

It's a time to bring out the creepy inside all us; but, what if the creepy really existed? What if bad things really did happen on Halloween night?

Not just scary stories to tell around a campfire but real bad things...true things, that forever changed those involved....murder, mayhem, and monsters...

What if they really do happen on Halloween?

Well, in this book we're going to take a look at some very scary, very disturbing things that really happened on Halloween night... where true crime meets the supernatural, where these shocking true stories are enough to make anyone who reads them NEVER go out on Halloween again...

TABLE OF CONTENTS

P.S. And Don't forget to Claim Your FREE
Bonuses After the Conclusion!

If you like **<u>FREE BOOKS on Creepy
True Ghost Stories</u>** –
come grab them here!! Free books each &
every week straight into your inbox!!

<u>www.mycreepybooks.com/</u>

Now, let's get down to those Creepy Halloween True Stories!!

Chapter 1: Hiding in the Closet

On Halloween 1977, Mr and Mrs Carter were not going out trick or treating. Their child was just 18 months old and too young to be able to understand the fun of Halloween.

In their home in Lawton, Comanche County Oklahoma, her mother put her down for the night in her crib at approximately 9 pm, and she and her husband went to bed not much later than that.

They slept in the front room of their small home. Their daughter meanwhile was sleeping soundly in her own bedroom.

When her parents woke early the next morning, mother Rose went to fetch their daughter from her crib. She was surprised that her daughter had not woken them during the night and was feeling very refreshed because of it.

Her happiness however turned to horror when she found her daughter's crib was empty. Her baby was gone.

Running to tell her husband, they both searched the house although they both knew their infant daughter could not have got out of the crib by herself. Frantic with worry, they called the Sherriff's office.

The police were quick to respond and once at the scene they checked the house for any possible signs of a break-in and forced entry.

No doors had been forced open and no windows broken. Everything was secure.

"I now believe that the person was already in her room, hiding in the closet," her father later told reporters, "What if we had opened the closet? What if we had gotten up to check her that night?

What if we had brought her in to sleep with us? What if? What if?" His torment was palpable.

Detectives at the scene had come up with this scenario as it seemed to be the only one that made sense to them – no doors or windows had been forced open and they did not believe the parents had anything to do with this baby disappearing.

Instead, a person had got into their house some time earlier than that night and had been hiding in the closet. It's like the most frightening horror movies – only this time it was true. It had really happened.

The parents were in total shock, fear, grief, terror – where was their little girl?

Who had hidden in the closet?

Why had they taken their baby?

What were they going to do with her?

They could barely get through each hour that she was missing. The police did their best – interviewing neighbors, friends, anyone but no-one had any information for them. No-one had heard or seen a thing.

No-one had seen the baby being carried out in the dead of night under cover of darkness on a night when many were out celebrating Halloween.

To the police, there was no motive either, and no trail to follow.

Then, more than 3 weeks later, their baby was found dead, lying beside a refrigerator in an abandoned house four blocks from the family home. Her 19-month-old body was badly decomposed.

A Fort Hood soldier had stumbled across her remains and reported it immediately to the police.

Detectives concluded that the baby had been placed inside the refrigerator by her kidnapper, shortly after her abduction, and left inside the refrigerator to suffocate.

Her body tumbled from her icy tomb when a group of neighborhood boys opened the refrigerator then fled in terror.

It appeared that her abductor, who had hidden in the closet of her room, had carried her out of her home and four blocks to the abandoned house and then purposely placed her inside the refrigerator to die.

Sealed inside the refrigerator, with no ability to open it herself, because she was just a baby, the baby was left to die inside as the airtight seal closed off any access to oxygen. It would also have muffled her screams.

It would not have taken her long to die. Her killer had to be a stone-cold psychopath.

The coroner determined that the baby had no injuries on her body and did not seem to have been harmed or assaulted in any way prior to being shut inside the refrigerator.

As for who would do this, and why, the detectives had no clues. At least, that was until they recalled a strikingly similar case, a year earlier….

3-year-old Mary Carpitcher and her twin sister Augustine had been snatched from their grandmother's home, only a few blocks away from where the now-dead baby had been found.

Missing for 48 hours, they were discovered by children playing near an abandoned house, who heard faint cries for help coming from somewhere in the house.

Searching all around it they tracked the source of the sound to the refrigerator, and inside they found the twin girls, one still alive but the other one dead.

The alive one had been in there for 10 days, trapped inside with her dead twin sister.

Shockingly, when the twin who had survived told detectives who had done it, they were led to a teenage girl called Jackie Roubideaux, a friend of their parents and a some-time babysitter for the twins when their parents went out for an evening.

She was well-liked and trusted by the twins' parents, who even sometimes took her to the movies with them when they were going.

On the day that the twins disappeared, this teenage girl had been at their home, playing with the girls, and later that day, a local woman said she had seen a girl resembling Jackie, dragging the two girls toward the abandoned house.

She thought nothing of it at the time, presuming the girls were mis-behaving and their ward was trying to keep them under control.

Jackie had also been babysitting them the night before their disappearance. She came from a poor family struggling to get by and she was the main carer for her sick mother and grandmother as well as babysitter for local kids.

Her life was not an easy one, but no-one in the neighbourhood would ever have believed she would have turned murderess.

Being the local neighbourhood baby-sitter, she also knew the other little girl who had ended up dead in a refrigerator – Nima Carter, because she babysat her too.

She didn't admit to it of course, and in fact, other than the testimony of the twin girl who had survived, who was just 3 years old, the police had no evidence or motive.

It took two years to bring the girl to trial for the murder of not one but two children and the attempted murder of a third.

With scant evidence however, Jackie received a hung jury verdict – they could not say for absolute certainty that she had done it.

The prosecution had called Sonja Bower and Della Clark, who were inmates in the Comanche County Jail with Miss Roubideaux. Both testified that Jackie admitted her guilt to them in early May 1981.

Bower said that she, Jackie and several other inmates were in a recreation area watching television. "I heard Jackie say, "Hell, yes, I did it and I'll get out of it,' " Bower said.

Jackie was brought to a second trial in 1983 for the murder of the twin girl who had died. – Prosecutors hoped they would have more luck this time, and although they couldn't prove she had killed Niman too, they believed in their own hearts she had.

They settled for the most likely conviction – the one with the eye-witness testimony from the surviving twin and to the satisfaction of the detectives, this time she did not get off with it. At the age of 24, she was finally found guilty of the cruel killing and sentenced to life.

She died of liver cancer in 2005. She always denied her guilt of both abductions, and she never said why she had done it. For the parents of both children who died, there was no real closure.

For parents who are reading this now, the fact is, sometimes there really are monsters hiding in the closet….

Chapter 2: The Snuff Movie

On Halloween 1981, the bodies of Elizabeth Platzman and Ronald Sisman were discovered in the apartment of Sisman, on the third floor at 207 West 22d Street, New York New York.

Both victims had been brutally savagely beaten, then shot in the head execution style, at close range.

His apartment had then been ransacked. The furniture was ripped open, drawers lay on the floor. It was as though whoever had killed them was searching for something too.

However, the apartment had no signs of forced entry. For the detectives, this clearly pointed to the possibility that the killer or killers had been let in; that this was someone one or both victims knew.

The young woman, Elizabeth Platzman, was a student at the nearby Smith College. She had moved in with Sisman some months ago. He was a photographer by trade, and was actually well-known in the avant-garde scene.

All was not what it seemed with him however; on the side he operated a shady business in producing pornography and selling cocaine.

At first, the detectives logically believed that his death and his girlfriends was probably a drug snatch gone wrong; that someone had got inside their apartment with the intention of stealing his supply of drugs and cash.

However, the more the cops looked into his background, the more they learned and the deeper the rabbit hole went.

Informers helped them to get a clearer picture of some of his criminal associates and word got to them that something had happened in prison that they should know about.

Ronald Sisman made snuff films they said, and his killer was after a snuff film stored in his apartment.

The story goes that this photographer was hired to film a killing so that it could be distributed for sale to a private individual who was a "high bidder," and the prison informant was none other than the man incarcerated for the "Son of Sam" murders!

The 'Son of Sam' murders had terrified New York at the time, in the summer of '77, and now David Berkowitz, the killer, was claiming that while he was killing "Son of Sam" victims Robert Violante and Stacy Moskowitz, Sisman was in a van parked close-by and was recording the killing on his video camera, to later be sold to the 'high bidder.'

Berkowitz said in prison that Sizman had a snuff film and "people" wanted it back. Berkowitz was serving life for the random shooting of six victims on the streets of New York but many believe he couldn't possible have acted alone.

In fact, he has often been accused of being a member of a satanic cult and of being at Uttemeyer Park when dogs were sacrificed in rituals by the 'cult.'

When Berkowitz had said in prison that Sizman would be getting "a visit," at his home, it could have just been "talk" but the thing was – he described the interior of Sizman's apartment to a Tee.

He'd also said that this 'visit,' would happen on Halloween and we all know, that this is supposed to be a night for Human Sacrifice among the worse satanic cults.

The detectives believe that "a group" visited Sizman that Halloween night – a group that he knew, and they wanted the copy of the snuff tape he had kept for himself – most likely as a tool for blackmail or 'currency.'

Berkowitz also spookily very accurately described details about the way in which they were killed – before they were killed. He described exactly what was going to happen to them if Sizman didn't surrender the "snuff" tape.

Who the killers were, and why Berkowitz could describe the particular manner of their deaths has never been fully solved, but it does seem to verify that the possibility of "Snuff films" really does exist… the filming of a real live person, or people being tortured and slaughtered for other people's viewing pleasure……

Chapter 3: Jewish Boy Mystery

Many orthodox Jews send their offspring to special religious schools called a Yeshiva, where they can learn the origins of the Jewish religion, which dates back over more than 5,000 years and is rich in rituals and the practice of Orthodox Judaism.

It was at one such Yeshiva, Mesivta high school in Long Beach, New York, on Halloween night of 1986, that a child was murdered.

A studious and popular 15-year-old Orthodox Jewish boy called Chaim Weiss had been found dead. Weiss was the son of prosperous New York business man Anton Weiss.

His son Chaim was one of just two students there who had their own room, at the request of their parents. Most of the boys shared dorms.

On the morning after Halloween, he was discovered dead in his room. There was blood everywhere. It looked like he had been bludgeoned to death with a hard object, most likely some sort of "hatchet" according to detectives.

He had also been stabbed multiple times in the head, and his spinal cord severed with a sharp blade.

The coroner later established that he died fairly quickly in the savage attack but whoever his killer was, they had carried out a sustained and frenzied attack on him after death too.

The walls of his bedroom were splattered with blood, brain fragments and soft tissue.

Veteran New York detective Don Daly was lead investigator on the grisly scene, along with crime scene investigators, who quickly deduced that, for some reason, the boy had been moved after death.

There was blood everywhere but no murder weapons. There was also no sign of a struggle.

The crime scene technicians suggested to the detective that the poor boy must have been attacked while he asleep in his bed, and then the killer had dragged his body from the bed and dumped it on the carpet.

The detective, on surveying the boy's bedroom noticed that a window was open. His bedroom door had not been broken down however, and the building supervisor told him that all doors, external and internal, had been locked as was procedure, during the night.

To the detective, this clearly pointed to an inside source – someone already in the building. His bedroom was on the third floor and it was not possible for the killer to have climbed in the boy's bedroom as it was on the 3rd floor.

All of the pupils and the staff were questioned and when no valid motive or suspect emerged, they were each subjected to a lie detector test. However, again no suspect emerged.

The detective obviously faced a huge dilemma. There was a dead boy and no suspect in the building.

A person out jogging early the morning of the boy's body being discovered said that they saw a young Jewish boy on a street close to the school, as he was running by.

Who this was, was never identified and so it could not be confirmed if this could have been the dead boy or one of his school pals, or if it even was true.

The detective was no closer to finding a motive nor a killer. He wondered if it was an anti-Semitic killing, a random victim chosen purely because he was

Orthodox Jew. There had been a fire earlier that year in the Temple only a couple of blocks away from the School.

An investigation by the Fire Marshals discovered that this fire was caused deliberately in an act of arson, although who set the fire was never found out.

Prior to this, at the boy's school a bed in the dorm had been found on fire. In this case, it could not be determined who had set the fire.

There was also the on-going harassment of the school boys occasionally in the area where the school was. Anti-Semitic feelings sometimes boiled over and the school had asked that this Halloween the boys should not wear their hats.

In the past, youths had harassed the school boys, knocking their hats from their heads or running off with them.

With this ruling passed down to the school boys, Halloween this year had passed without those incidents taking place; and yet instead, there now had been the most savage murder in their school.

Could this too have been a random act of anti-Semitism too? – The problem with this was that the bedroom of the dead boy was on the third floor and for a person off the street to reach it, they would have had to go through the dorms occupied by all the other school boys who shared the dorms.

The bedrooms of the staff too would have to have been passed by the intruder. This would have been an audacious risk for the intruder – he could have been caught at any time if one of the boys had woken in the night as he was passing their beds.

Also, if the intruder had wanted to randomly attack a Jewish boy – he had closer targets than the boy in his own bedroom – although, attacking one of the boys in the dorm would have resulted in all of the boys waking up because of the savagery of the intruder's attack, they surely would have heard it.

Although the boy who was killed hadn't screamed – he'd been killed by the axe-like weapon before he'd even had a chance to wake up and try to defend himself.

The other odd thing about the case was that the coroner worked out that the young boy's body had been moved up to 45 minutes after he was killed – had the killer stayed in his bedroom, at the risk of getting caught, for over 45 minutes?

Or, perhaps more likely, had the killer been inside the building all the time?

Was the killer actually one of the people supposed to be inside the building? Was it a student, a teacher? – But they had all passed lie detector tests!

There was one thing which also pointed to the killer being someone who was already inside the building, someone who belonged at the school – this was the fact that something at the crime scene suggested the killer was very well versed in Orthodox Jewish Practices and traditions.

In Orthodox Jewish death customs and rites, a window where the person died would commonly be opened; in the belief that this allowed the soul of the dead person to depart.

It was unlikely the boy had opened the window before he had gone to bed or during the night, because it was a cold Halloween night.

Another ritual gave another clue; One of the school rabbis asked to leave a memorial candle in the boy's room, and for it to burn for seven days straight.

This was arranged and the crime scene was then sealed.

No-one was to be allowed to enter the boy's room. So how, two days later, had another candle mysteriously appeared in his bedroom?

Detective Daly said that no one in the school ever admitted to placing that second candle in the boy's bedroom: "If they lit that candle as a gesture of sympathy or display of love for the boy, why wouldn't they come forward and say that? But nobody came forward with that."

In summarizing the puzzling case, the detective said: "There were a lot of questions that haven't been answered. No leads. Nothing from outside – which is unusual."

Does he feel it was an insider? – it sure sounds like it could be his opinion.

Was it one of the pupils? One of his Rabbi's?

Or, could someone have got in the building and pulled it off?

Why was he chosen? Why was he killed?

We still do not know. All we do know is that someone sneaked into that boy's room on Halloween night and virtually decapitated the young boy, stabbed him multiple times after death, and left open a window in his bedroom so that his soul could be taken to Heaven.

All in all, it is a bizarre and real tragic case of Halloween murder.

Despite the many years that have since passed, the killer of the young boy has never been caught.

This Halloween killer got clean away with his crime. For the boy's parents, the tragedy lives on; "The not knowing makes it much more difficult for me to cope," said his father.

"Certain things I accept; My son is dead. But the murderer is still loose. All these unanswered questions make me feel very, very uneasy."

Chapter 4: The Bunny Girl who disappeared on Halloween.

Hyun Jong Song was raised in the South Korean capital of Seoul, but she emigrated with her parents to the United States in the 1950's.

They settled in Springfield, Virginia. The young girl was happy to be in a new country, one that was more liberal than her homeland and she enjoyed attending a new high school, where her friends called her 'Cindy.'

After graduating high school, she went to Penn State University to study arts and she lived in an apartment very close to the university campus. She was a friendly and popular girl, well-liked by her peers.

In fact, she was often the centre of attention, as she had a vivacious and out-going personality that people were drawn to.

In October 2001, she was in her final year of studies, just months away from graduating. She was an active participant in both her classes and the wealth of social activities available for students to do there.

On this October, Cindy was invited to go to Halloween party at the nearby Players' Nightclub. Everyone was going to dress-up for the night and after finding it hard to decide what costume to wear, Cindy settled on a Bunny-Girl outfit.

She purchased a pink shirt with a rabbit logo on it, teamed this with a tennis skirt and added knee-length boots and a red jacket. Then she added the bunny ears. That night she also took with her a small backpack for her personal items.

She arrived at the nightclub with her friends and they partied until past 2 a.m. Then she left and went back to one of her friend's near-by apartments, and they sat up drinking and chatting and having fun for a couple more hours.

When she left her friend's apartment, they later described her as 'mildly intoxicated, but not drunk.'

She didn't leave alone – another friend drove her back to her apartment close to the college campus.

Her friend stopped the car right outside her apartment and Cindy got out. Her friend watched until Cindy had gone inside the building, and then they drove away. It was now around 4 a.m.

This would be the last time anyone saw Cindy alive. On November 4th, her friends reported to the police that she was missing.

No one had seen or heard of her since the Halloween night.

The police arrived at her apartment but when they entered it, they could find no sign of Cindy and nor could they find any clues that might explain where she had gone.

Inside her apartment was her back-pack from the night of the Halloween party, and her cell phone.

They even noticed that a pair of false eyelashes were in her bathroom – and she had worn these on the night of the Halloween party, so it was safe for the police to assume that she had made it back to her apartment... but where was she now?

There was also no sign of a forced entry, and no sign of any struggle. There was nothing at all inside the apartment that would suggest someone else had been there, someone unwelcome.

Her purse was gone however, and so too was her driving licence, car keys and apartment keys.

In the course of their immediate inquiries, the police questioned those closest to her – her friends at college, and a boyfriend she had just split from – who had been a long-term boyfriend.

The police wondered, could she have been so heartbroken over the split that she had killed herself?

Had her ex-boyfriend anything to do with her unexplained disappearance? But her friends told the police that she was not heartbroken and the split had been a mutual thing. Both her and her ex-boyfriend were cool about it they said.

The police did find her diary – still at her apartment and through reading this diary they discovered that

Cindy occasionally dabbled in drug experimentation, including ecstasy.

Her friends denied that they had taken any drugs on the night of the Halloween party though.

The trail appeared to be completely cold for the police – they had no leads no credible suspect and no clue where she was.

They did receive one interesting tip from a woman who said she had seen the missing woman – but this was not near her apartment.

The woman lived nearly 200 kilometres away! but she said she had seen the young woman shouting out from inside of a moving car, and said that she was calling for someone to help her.

The driver of the car, said this witness, threatened her and the girl in the car with violence to shut them up.

Then he drove away, with the young woman still in the car, and the witness sincerely believed she was being held against her will. She fitted Cindy's physical description.   This was in the City's Chinatown district.

When the police asked the witness for further details however, this witness changed her story and then clammed up – perhaps she was lying, or, perhaps she was too scared to talk.

The police discovered that a taxi company that operated locally had dropped a passenger off outside the missing woman's apartment at 3.57 a.m. just three minutes before Cindy herself was dropped off there.

Unfortunately, however, the company kept no record of who their passengers were and so they were unable to even give a description of this person.

The case of this young woman who had vanished on Halloween night was publicized widely, in both the local media and state wide but no-one ever came forward to say that they had been the passenger in the taxi that night.

Her family flew over from South Korea to assist in the search for her, but despite this and the on-going police search, no sign of her was found.

Fast forward to 2005, four years after the event, a convicted bank robber named Hugo Selenski claimed that he and a friend, Michael Kerkowski, saw Cindy out in the early hours of that morning and seeing her dressed up as a bunny girl, he said they assumed she was a prostitute.

He said they abducted her and took her back to their apartment, where they kept her for a while, imprisoning her in a walk-in safe, but that she died in a way that he did not explain.

He refused to go into details about it. He says that after she died, they took her body to the Luzerne County and buried her.

It didn't end there however – Selenski says he then killed his friend after discovering that Kerkowski had kept the young woman's bunny ears as a 'trophy.'

Despite this grisly story, the police could not find real evidence to back up this account.

In fact, informants told the police that it was more likely Selenski who had killed her- in fact, he had boasted to several people about killing her himself. And, there was the small matter of dead bodies being found at his property!

Two drug-dealers had been killed and buried on his property; and they weren't the only ones – between five to fourteen sets of human remains were discovered buried on his property – but, none of these belonged to the missing young woman.

If he did do it, then he buried her body elsewhere.

The truth of what happened to Cindy that night has still to be revealed. She has tragically never been found.…

Chapter 5: Vanished

Exactly a year after Cindy disappeared on Halloween night, this time it was a college boy who disappeared.

He too had been attending a Halloween party, and he too was wearing a Halloween costume. This time, it happened in the city of Minneapolis.

21-year-old Chris Jenkins was out at a Bar with friends, partying on Halloween Night 2002.

Jenkins was an honor student at the University of Minnesota's prestigious Carlson School of Management and he had high hopes for a successful future in the world of Finance when he graduated.

Like Cindy, he was a popular, outgoing and well-liked young man who had many friends. He was on several sports teams including the Lacrosse Team at college.

He was making the most of his final year before job rounds and interviews started and he was fully enjoying all the social activities his college had to offer.

On this Halloween night, he was at a Bar called the Lone Tree Bar & Grill in downtown Minneapolis. When midnight came around, everyone had been having a hoot and the drink was flowing and Jenkins found himself being told by the bouncer to get out, telling him he was causing a problem.

The bouncer was an off-duty cop and although Jenkins protested, the cop insisted he leave the premises. His friends later said he did nothing to justify getting thrown out.

Outside the Bar, Jenkins stood there in a Native American fancy dress costume, with a big feather headdress. What he didn't have was his wallet – the cop had thrown him out without letting him fetch his wallet, car keys or apartment keys.

He was stranded outside with nothing to get home with. Plus, it was a freezing night. He had on just a light weight cotton Native American outfit.

With no way to get home, and no way to call anyone, he must have been standing there trying to decide what to do. But he didn't stand there for long. He couldn't have; because shortly afterward he disappeared, and so began his unexplained disappearance.

After that weekend, his parents discovered that he'd never made it back to his college apartment. His friends called them, concerned that they did not know where he was.

His parents called the police and a search for their missing son began.

Police conducted Investigations by interviewing staff who worked at the bar, the off-duty police bouncers, all of his friends, and anyone else they thought might be able to help them in some way explain how and why he had vanished.

The police believed that the most likely scenario was he had walked across the wide Hennepin Avenue Bridge, that would lead in the direction of his college apartment.

No one seemed to have seen him after he was thrown out of the bar.

The police heard that his girlfriend had been friendly with one of the cops on bouncer-duty at the bar and in fact she had left with him that night, but there was no evidence to suggest that either the girlfriend or the cop had anything to do with the college boy vanishing.

The police investigation and search for Jenkins was thorough but as the days turned into weeks they came no nearer to finding him nor determining where he had gone or what had happened to him.

Four months later, his body was spotted in the Mississippi River, floating in his Native American costume. The police concluded that he had died as a result of falling into the river; or he had jumped in and killed himself.

His heartbroken parents however disagreed with both options. He had nothing to be depressed about they insisted and, there was no way he could have simply "fallen in" the Mississippi.

It just didn't make sense to them; but with the police still calling it an "accident," they hired a private eye to help them and scent dogs too.

This scent dogs led the private eye to parking garage not far from the Bar he had been in. There were blood drops at the parking garage – and, they matched Jenkin's blood.

His parents had been saying to the police that their son could not have killed himself or fallen in – he was found floating on his back and he had his arms crossed over his chest – they hired forensic experts who had told them that no drowning person drowns on their back with their arms folded over their chest as though they are perfectly at peace

A person drowning struggles and flails even if they are trying to kill themselves, the experts said, as it is a natural instinct.

In fact, forensic experts also discovered that he had no water in his lungs – which would be impossible if he had drowned.

This meant that he was dead before he got in the water – a completely different scenario to what the police were saying. He was murdered.

He didn't die by accident. He was murdered and then put in the river after he was dead. His parents hired esteemed pathologist Dr. Michael Baden. He has been an expert witness in many controversial trials and he examined the body of their son through the autopsy notes and he determined that this was no "accidental drowning."

He was insistent that their son died before entering the river. The parents of the victim also reviewed the cctv footage at the bridge and despite what the police said, they found no images of their son walking across the bridge – he had not done so. Instead, he had been taken to a garage and then driven away.

How did he die?

Who killed him?

Well, for several years the police refused to change his cause of death to murder. After changing it to murder, on the continued persistence of his parents, the police are still no closer to finding out who killed him.

His mother says he was abducted and killed. She doesn't know why, or by who, but she knows he suffered enormously before they killed him. A professor Lee Gilberston, member of the criminal justice faculty at St. Cloud State University in Minnesota says Jenkins is not the only victim.

He claims there's at least 40 more men, who have all ended up the same way, mostly college men, across the country, but the police think they are "accidents" and don't take what he says seriously.

Chillingly, the professor says, the "killers" leave "Smiley-Face" Graffiti at the scene each time...he says it has been happening for many years now.

College men, abducted, and killed, then dumped in rivers across the country……he says families have no idea what is really going on and he adds, that it shows no sign ending anytime soon.

No-one knows who the "The Smiley Face Killers" are.

Chapter 6: Orange Socks Halloween Murder.

In this next case, we have yet another refence to clothing and yet this victim was not wearing a Halloween fancy dress costume – but still, she too came to great harm on Halloween night.

It happened on Halloween back in 1979, when her life abruptly and unexpectedly ended.

She was murdered and her body dumped in a ditch along Interstate 35 in Georgetown, Texas, and despite widespread media coverage of her murder at the time and for many years afterwards, no-one has ever come forward to identify her.

Which is why she becoming known simply as the "Orange Socks" girl, because of the orange-colored socks she was wearing on the night of her evil murder.

In fact, her socks were the only items of clothing left on her body – she was found naked except for these.

One of the difficulties in finding out who killed her was that where she was found was a major route through Texas; it was used by travellers in cars, and in trucks.

Interstate winds its way across the Unites States, from close to the Mexican border in the south, through Minnesota, close to where Chris Jenkins in the previous story was murdered and up to the Canadian border.

On Halloween 1979, a trucker pulled off the route, a few miles short of the county line, and pulled into the truck stop outside of Georgetown, Texas to rest for a while.

As he disembarked from his cab to go take a walk and stretch his legs, his eyes were immediately drawn to something unexpected close-by.

There was something lying in the culvert beside the road. At first, he thought he must be seeing things – he could see a shop mannequin, lying discarded by the side of the road, but then as he got closer to it, not quite sure, he recoiled in horror as he realized that this shop mannequin was in fact a woman's body, lying naked and quite clearly dead.

He rushed to alert the Sheriff's from Williamson County, who arrived quickly. Examining the woman's body, it did not take long to notice that she had been badly beaten.

Her body bore significant bruising and it appeared she had sustained a savage attack by person or person's unknown.

Around her throat were purple marks that seemed to point to her cause of death being strangulation. She was entirely naked, except for her bright orange socks.

The rest of her clothing was gone and so too were any other personal belongings. There was nothing to use to identify her with.

The only thing the police found at the scene was a matchbook lying close to her body. It said, 'Holiday Inn' at Henryetta, Oklahoma. This location was over 5 hours away from where they were.

She was 5ft 8 inches, approximately 150lbs, with pierced ears, a small scar under her chin, and two of her teeth were missing. She wore a thin silver ring with a pearl.

When her body was examined by the county coroner, he confirmed that she had indeed been strangled to death, and he estimated that this had occurred just hours before the truck driver had spotted her body lying in the culvert.

Her injuries did not end there however; the coroner determined that before she had been strangled, she had been raped.

She had then been dragged by persons unknown, across the highway and then thrown over the guard rail – to the drop below.

Whoever had done this, had been callous in the extreme, as well as extremely violent. They had attacked her with savage rage.

However, her face was still recognisable and in their attempt to identify her, the police offered photographs of her to the local press.

No-one came forward to claim her as theirs however; no parents, no siblings, no friends.

The only response the Sheriff had was a phone call from an anonymous woman, who phoned them not once but three times in total. The anonymous woman said that she had seen the victim hitchhiking in the area in which her body had been found and on the same day that she was believed to have been killed.

The anonymous woman refused to give her name however, and the police were unable to trace her, to question her further.

The woman lying dead in the County morgue was to remain unclaimed and unidentified for weeks, which turned into months, which turned into years.

Because of the amount of traffic that passed through the spot where she was found, it was impossible for the Sheriffs to pin-point a possible suspect in her murder; thousands of truckers would pass by each day alone.

The police had no leads no clues no evidence and no suspects, at all.

Then, four years later, a man called Henry Lee Lucas, who I'm sure most readers will recognise the name, was arrested by Texan police for unlawful possession of a firearm.

Henry Lee Lucas had already been on their radar as a suspect in the murder of a wealthy lady, eighty-two-year-old aged and infirm Kate Rich.

He would of course be accused and convicted of many heinous murders, but he confessed that not only had he killed approximately 300 people, he was the killer of "Orange Socks" too.

He told the authorities that her name was Judy and that he had picked her up when she was hitch-hiking, in Oklahoma.

He said that he asked her for sex when they were near Georgetown, but she refused him.

As a consequence of refusing to have sex with him, he throttled her, dragged her naked body across the highway and threw her over the side of the guardrail into the culvert below.

The authorities took his confession very seriously and they took him to the spot where her body was found.

Lucas then showed the authorities how he had dragged her naked body along the gravel of the road.

The police were convinced of his confession and he was in fact sentenced and found guilty of her murder. He was sentenced to death.

However, notwithstanding Henry Lee Lucas being one of the worst monsters to have ever lived, not everyone is convinced that he did it. After all, he said he'd killed 300 others too, but in most of these confessions, he was proven to be lying.

In "Orange Sock" case, he was even believed to have been employed in a different state at the time she was killed.

In fact, for it to be true, he would have to have driven non-stop at approximately 80 mph, from Florida to Oklahoma to Texas and then back to Florida in his off-time from work – it just seemed a little unfeasible.

In fact, some sleuths even took the time to try to replicate the journey he would have had to make and not one of them could complete the round trip in the time necessary for it to be true.

Things got even worse for the veracity of his confession when it also came out later that one of the police officers on the case had shown him some of the crime scene photos taken when she'd been found.

This explained why and how Lucas had been able to give details about her body and the condition and position it had been found in – it wasn't necessarily because he'd been there personally, but it was because he'd already seen pcitures of it.

These factors and several other anomalies led to his conviction for the rape and murder of "Orange Socks" being overturned.

The former President, George Bush senior was the one to quash his death sentence.

Despite many of the Missing Person's registers listing "Orange Socks" on their websites, and the case appearing on America's Most Wanted, she still has not been identified nor has her killer ever been captured.

Was he one of the thousands of truckers who used that road every day?

Or, someone else?

As a result of past or subsequent murders, the killing of "Orange Socks" has sometimes been linked to these other cases. For example, 17-year-old Martha Marie Morrison was last seen at her apartment in Arizona in October 1974, where she was enrolled in a Jobs Corps program. She looked very similar to "Orange Socks."

In fact, artist's impressions showed they bore an uncanny likeness. Her remains were found in Vancouver, Washington.

"Orange Socks" was also compared with other missing person's cases with the suggestion that perhaps she was one of these other missing young women, including Pinkie Davis-Heron, 18, who vanished one evening the same years as "Orange Socks", after visiting friends, in Delvalle, Texas.

But DNA ruled this out, as also did the possibility that it could be Nancy Jason who went missing in Chevy Chase, Maryland in 1977, and Kathleen Rodgers, 15, who vanished from Oroville, California a year before. She was none of these victims.

How could a young woman disappear and be murdered but no one notice her missing?

No-one has ever come forward to say that they know who she is or whose family she once belonged to.

But perhaps much more chilling is the fact that her killer also has never been caught either.....

Has he killed again?

Is he still on the loose?

Chapter 7: Jane doe

Another Halloween murder happened six years later, again in Texas. This time it was Huntersville, Walker County, Texas. Remember this; a killer was still on the loose after the murder of "Orange Socks."

Huntersville is approximately 150 miles from where "Orange Socks" was found, but that's not far in a truck or car...

Huntersville resides on the edge of the Sam Houston National Forest, a scenic part of the country but intersected by route 45 interstate, which takes a traveller from Dallas to Houston.

On Halloween 1980, a truck driver was en-route along Interstate 45 when he decided to pull over for a short break, on the outskirts of Huntsville.

In an eerily coincidental manner, as he disembarked from his cab, he spotted something lying by the side of the road. It looked like a shop mannequin.

As he walked closer however, he too, just like the other trucker, recoiled in horror when he realized that this mannequin was in fact a naked dead woman.

The arriving Sheriffs were quick to see the similarity to "Orange Socks." This victim was also a young woman, naked, and raped and beaten.

She too had been viciously beaten, savagely raped, and then dragged across the tarmac and thrown over the guardrail. The only difference was, she had a bite mark on her back.

She was 5ft 5inches, 115 lbs, brown eyes, brown hair and had a small scar above her eyebrow. From the condition of her teeth and her healthy weight the coroner determined she was probably from a middle-class family.

Her toenails were painted pink and she wore a pendant necklace. While her clothes were missing, the sheriffs did locate her sandals nearby or at least, they assumed they were hers due to the proximity of her body.

No other items were found however – no purse or i.d. This time however, the authorities were fortunate enough to locate some witnesses who had met this woman before she had died.

One of the witnesses was the manager of the South End Gulls Service Station who told them that a young woman had been dropped off at the Service Station by a man who was driving a blue Chevrolet.

He described the young woman as wearing a pair of jeans and a pale cardigan or pullover and said that she had been asking about how to get to the nearby prison, Ellis Prison Farm.

This was a high-security prison operated by the Department of Corrections and it housed some of the country's worst offenders including those on death row.

The Service Station Manager told police that after the girl got directions to the prison she set off on foot (although this would have been a very long walk as it was several miles away.)

She was next seen at the truck stop further north on route 145, where again a witness came forward to say that he had seen her and she had been asking for directions to the Prison. The witness this time was a waitress at the Pit stop.

The waitress said that she disclosed to her that she was going to visit someone in the prison and that she came from Rockport.

The waitress didn't think the girl was telling her the complete truth – she thought she looked younger than the age she had given, of 19 years old.

The waitress, who was concerned for the girl's well-being, even inquired if her parents knew she was out here, and the young woman replied, "Who cares!"

The waitress said she then took off on foot, walking, with the intention of walking or hitching to the prison.

That was the last witness to see her alive. The next morning her body was mistaken for a shop mannequin as it lay discarded by the road side.

On learning of this conversation, the police went straight away to the Prison, and a photograph of the dead woman was circulated among the prisoners.

The police were sure one of them would come forward to say they knew her, but none did. Not one of them admitted knowing her.

They checked with the personnel too who worked there, but they also had no idea who this young woman was. It's possible of course that one of the prisoners did know but was not willing to come forward.

For this young woman, she too was now given a nickname; "Walker County Jane Does," as no-one knew who she was.

The trail went completely cold. No-one missed her, or at least, no one came forward to say so.

The police of course were wondering whether her death had been at the same hands as that of "Orange Socks" because after all, they had both been savagely beaten, raped and left naked by the roadside after strangulation; but they still had no suspects for either victim.

Fast forward then to 1999 and her body was exhumed so that new advances in DNA could perhaps help to solve her identity.

The new tests would be able to determine more accurately what her age had been.

In 2015, the Walker County Sheriff's Office re-opened the case. Appeals for information had been sent out and the Sheriff was hopeful for a new break in the case.

But it only led to more confusion; her potential identity has been suggested to be Maria Anjiras, a teen who ran away from home in Grand Prairie, Texas, or Deborah McCall who was last seen leaving school in Illinois.

Nor Kristy Booth who was a waitress in Midland, Texas, and who was last seen leaving the restaurant she worked at to go home, or Cindy King, who vanished from home in Oregon and had a similar scar above her eyebrow to "Walker County Jane Doe.

These young women have been ruled out, because of DNA testing, but still no answer have been found to explain who "Jane Doe" is.

Chapter 8: Baby GONE

When Marilyn Damman, 24, set out on a shopping trip in East Meadow, Nassau County New York, on Halloween 1955, she was in a hurry.

She pushed her 7-month-old infant daughter Pamela in her baby carriage as her toddler 2 ½ year old Steven walked by her side.

She was hurrying to the supermarket on Merrick Avenue, where she usually went to buy her basic groceries such as milk and bread.

She arrived at approximately 2.30 p.m. and to her dismay she discovered it was rather packed with other shoppers.

The thought of pushing her way through with a baby carriage and her small son did not appeal to her and she thought the best thing to do would be to leave the baby carriage outside of the supermarket and to leave her son there with it.

She only needed one item of shopping that day and so she couldn't see the point of struggling inside with her two children. So, she told her young son that she would be back in a couple of minutes and she darted inside.

Taking only a very short amount of time to purchase her grocery, she emerged from the shop relieved that she had chosen not to bother bringing the children inside with her, but she found herself turning from side to side on the sidewalk, checking her location and feeling rather confused.

That confusion very quickly turned to panic and then hysteria. The baby carriage and her young son were nowhere to be seen.

They were gone. There was no sign of them. Fortunately for her a passing policeman noticed her growing distress and stopped to inquire what was wrong.

Immediately understanding her situation, he summoned other officers and an alert was sent out to all patrolmen in the area to search for the missing children.

As the police cars cruised the streets urgently searching for her children, to her surprise a few moments later one of the cars spotted a baby carriage outside one of the stores nearby.

The cops quickly ran over to it and found to their relief, the missing baby fast asleep inside, blissfully unaware of the drama that had unfolded.

The problem was that although she was absolutely fine, the baby carriage was on its own – her brother was no-where to be seen. The 18-month-old little boy was gone!

The police returned the baby to its mother but their search now was far from over. By the close of day, up to 5,000 personnel from the city law enforcement, fire men, and volunteers had joined in the search for the little boy.

He seemed to have simply vanished from the busy streets.

That night and the next two days passed with all the personal in law enforcement still trying to find the missing boy, but there was no sign of him.

The police were forced to change his status from missing to possible abduction. They continued looking for him of course, but they had no leads to go on.

No-one had come forward with any information about seeing the boy or seeing any one with him either.

Days grew into weeks and then into months and the little boy was still missing.

The police turned first to local hospital records to check on parents who had suffered bereavements through the death of their own children, especially any whose children had died young.

The police wondered, could a grieving parent have snatched him off the street to try to make up for the loss of their own child?

The detective assigned to the case asked his parents to speak to the newspaper reporters and the TV stations.

They wanted as much publicity as possible about his disappearance, hoping that someone, somewhere would come forward with information.

Although they had re-classified his case to abduction, they had received no ransom demand and couldn't say for sure that he had been kidnapped, but this seemed the most realistic scenario to them.

One lead that came from this was a realtor, who came forward to say that they believed they had seen the little boy in Brooklyn, holding the hand of a woman.

Unfortunately, without any idea who this woman was, the police could do nothing with this, and of course, they had no proof that it was the missing boy either.

A few weeks pass by and the parents then received a letter in the mail. It was a ransom note. It demanded $3,000 for the safe return of their son.

A short while passed and they received another letter. This time the ransom was $10,000 for the safe return of their son. Again, this letter did not give any details about how this money should be paid, or where, or to who.

Then came a third ransom demand letter, this time upping the money to $14,000. The parents would have complied; they would have done anything to get their little boy back, but, detectives discovered that the author of these three ransom notes was in fact a college student who was acting as an opportunist with his eye on some easy money and he had no idea where the little boy was.

Student Robert Fontaine, living in New York, had nothing at all to do with the disappearance of their son. The FBI arrested him and he was charged with extortion.

In May of the following year, a small boy was found abandoned at a Gas Station in Arizona.

Unfortunately, what looked like a promising sign turned out to be another abandoned boy but nothing to do with the missing one.

This child had been dumped at the Gas Station by parents who could no longer cope with looking after him because he had development difficulties.

Fifteen months after he went missing, in February 1957, an outdoorsman who was checking animal traps in the woods in Fox Chase, PA, came across a hideous discovery.

He found a body, wrapped in a blanket and placed inside a cardboard box. He ran off to summon the police. When local investigators arrived, they were as heartbroken as the outdoorsman to see the pitiful state of the deceased child.

The county coroner examined the remains of the little boy and determined that he was a blue-eyed blonde-haired boy, approximately 5 years old.

This would rule him out from being the missing boy Steven, although eerily, he had a scar in his chin in almost exactly the same spot as Steven.

However, the child in the cardboard box had never broken any bones in his short life, whereas Steven had broken an arm as a baby.

The case of the little boy found in the woods in the cardboard became known famously as "the Boy in the Box," and tragically his identity was never discovered.

More than fifty years later, in 2009, the case of missing Steven took on a very strange twist. A man who lived in Michigan, by the name of John Barnes, claimed that he was Steven.

Barnes was an out of work laborer who went on to explain that he was born in the same year as Steven, although he said he had lost his birth certificate, but he explained that he had always had a feeling that his "parents" were not his real parents. Indeed.

This seemed to be confirmed on his mother's death bed when he said she told him she was not his biological mother. He added that he bore no physical resemblance to either his mother or father.

He contacted the missing boy's mother and began corresponding with her, telling her that he was sure he was her now-grown up son.

But, when DNA tests were conducted, it proved conclusively that this laborer was not related at all to the family and was certainly not the missing son.

As for the fate of little Steven, we sadly will probably never know what happened to him and perhaps it would be best that we will not know. His fate perhaps was one we would not like to know the details of.

Could he still be alive today? Perhaps there could be a happy ending. Perhaps he lost his memory shortly after his disappearance, perhaps someone took him in, someone who had no idea that the police were looking for him…..but that doesn't really make sense does it ….?

Chapter 9: Bad Surprise!

In September 1957, in the small farming community of Utica, Kansas, English teacher Betty Stevens and Principal William Hobert Sallee devised something that they believed would be great fun for their students this Halloween. different for their students.

So, on the night of Halloween, Betty led them all to an abandoned farmhouse, a couple mile outside of town.

What her students didn't know was that she and other teachers had decorated the dilapidated farmhouse as a haunted house for a party.

The centrepiece of this surprise party was their Principal, William Sallee, who would pretend to be hanging in the middle of one of the rooms in the dark, covered in ketchup to pretend it was blood.

When the students reached the dark room in which he was hanging the students did indeed get a shock – he was moaning and struggling and then he appeared to be hanging limply. It was very realistic.

In fact, it was a masterful performance that convinced each of the students, who thought it was the most frightening and awesome thing they'd ever seen!

But when Betty approached the Principal of the school to take a close-up photo of him hanging there, she made a shocking discovery - he had slipped, and this had caused the noose to automatically tighten around his neck.

The moaning and the struggling and the Principal going limp hadn't been acting at all - the students had actually been witnessing his slow, painful and terrible death....

If you like **<u>FREE BOOKS on Creepy</u>**

<u>True Ghost Stories</u> –

come grab them here!!

Free books each & every week straight into your inbox!!

<u>www.mycreepybooks.com</u>

Want Some

FREE CREEPY BOOKS

Every Week???

- Yes, really! We send out FREE Creepy Books to our Subscribers every single Week!! – If you think that sounds pretty AWESOME, all you need to do is Sign Up!! – It's that easy!!

Subscribe here:

www.mycreepybooks.com

We love giving out CREEPY Books away FREE to our Loyal Readers - & all you have to do is keep an eye on your Inbox for all your FREE CREEPY Books ever single week!

www.mycreepybooks.com

p.s. if you enjoyed this book of chilling stories, please could you leave us a review on Amazon?

This helps us get these books in front of more people who love true ghost tales!!

Thank you so much, you are so awesome!!!!

EXCERPTS from the Creepy True Ghost Stories Books by the authors at Bloody Moon Publishing

The World's Creepiest True Ghost Tales
By Roger P. Hunt

Chapter 4: Arianna Grande and the Portal to Hell

Arianna Grande is loved and admired by millions of fans, particularly after she so bravely returned to the Manchester Arena in England after her concert suffered unbelievable tragedy with the bombing and killing of 22 concert-goers, on May 22nd, 2017.

Despite this mass-murder happening while she was in the concert arena, having just finished her concert, she bravely returned a month later to host and sing in a tribute concert to the victims.

It could not have been easy to return to the place that had seen such horror and death, and she bravely faced up to the possible threat that it could happen again, and performed all night for the grieving fans and families of the victims.

Perhaps what is less known about Arianne Grande is the supernatural intrusion she has been facing in her life, as she explains herself when being interviewed by Complex Magazine.

She said; "We were in Kansas City a few weeks ago and we went to this haunted castle. We were so excited. Then the next night we wanted to go to Stull Cemetery, which is known as one of the seven gates to hell on Earth."

Ariana mysteriously went on to explain that, while en-route to the cemetery in their car she became aware of a number of strange and unexplained phenomena, which to her signalled that a demon was close and horrors were afoot.

"I felt this sick, overwhelming feeling of negativity and we smelled sulphur, which is the sign of a demon, and there was a fly in the car randomly, which is another sign of a demon."

This was just the beginning. Strange thoughts began to enter her head; thoughts that were not her own. "It was like; What if we wore masks to the grocery store?"

This worried her a lot – why would she think something like that? And, she started to become increasingly more concerned the closer they got to the alleged Portal to Hell.

Grande took it so seriously that she even lowered the car's window and apologized aloud to having disrupted the demons who dwelled there. "We are sorry! We did not mean to disrupt your peace," she told them aloud.

It seems that before this incident, Grande had read up quite a bit on supernatural phenomenon, including demonic encounters, and she knew that these signs were enough to cause her fear.

They must be careful, she knew now. But she couldn't resist getting out at the cemetery to take a selfie.

Later, when she reviewed the snap she had taken, that was when the Goosebumps rose on her arms.

"There are three super distinct faces in the picture," she confides. Demonic faces.

She truly now hoped that the apology she had said aloud on leaving the cemetery would be enough to protect her. But unfortunately, this just wasn't the case.

"The next day, I tried to send the picture to my manager, and it said, "This file can't be sent; it's 666 megabytes. - I'm not kidding."
Things were about to get much worse however.

"I was going to sleep about two weeks ago. I had just gotten off the phone and as soon as I closed my eyes I heard this really loud rumble right by my head.

When I opened my eyes, it stopped immediately, but when I closed my eyes it started again, with whispers.

Every time I closed my eyes I started seeing these really disturbing images with like, red shapes."

When she opened her eyes, "There was this massive black matter. I don't know what it was but I watched it move to the front of my bed. I started crying."

Terrified, she grabbed her phone and quickly described the horror unfolding around her to a friend, screaming into the receiver; "What should I do, what should I do?"

Her friend didn't know what to tell her to do and said; "Tell it to go!"

Grande, out of fear and knowing that these entities wanted respect, was too scared of the repercussions if she told it to leave, but she also had the presence of mind to remember that demons will feed of a person's fear; they like to cause fear so that they can drink in that fear and feed off it.

She knew she had to try to remain as calm as possible and so again, showing the great bravery she is becoming known for, she resolutely made the decision not to project any of her fear or negative worries outward for the demon to feed on.

She did her absolute best to remain calm and to think of anything positive she could think of – she wanted to try to drive the demon away with positive thoughts and ignore the whispering she had heard in her ear, ignore the evil things the demon had been whispering to her, trying to influence her, trying to get her to enjoy the evil just like it enjoyed it.

She faced a terrible battle that night alone in the hotel room and one can only marvel at this young woman's courage and she explains that after this period of facing off the "black mass" and the eerily terrifying whispers of the demon, the last thing she remembers was seeing that cloud of darkness fading as she fell asleep.

To her immense relief, when she woke it was morning, and the black entity was gone.

Did Arianna Grande accidentally free a demon entity from the portal of Hell when she went to the Cemetery?

Will it return to her again, to torment her…?

Will she always be plagued by evil entering her life to torment her and terrify her?

The Jikininki - Corpse Eating Demons

In Japan, there are many types of spirits that are believed to haunt the living. One such spirit is a terrible one called the Jikininki, who is a demon that enjoys causing terror and pain to its victims.

Horrifically, the Jikininki are man-eating demons. They feed on human corpses.

According to Japanese tradition, these evil entities loot the graveyards of Japan, and people who claim to have had the misfortune of encountering one alone in a graveyard when visiting a dead relative have said that it resembles a decomposing corpse, with long sharp claws.

If the Jikininki cannot steal a freshly buried body, it will often steal a pet to consume.

According to legend the Jikininki first appeared to Muso Kokushi, a travelling Buddhist. While he was traveling alone in the mountains, he lost his way. Wear and very hungry, he thought he saw in the distance a tiny house which belonged to a priest.

He hoped he could make it there, and when he reached it, he asked the priest if he could stay there the night.

Unfortunately for him, the priest told him he could not stay there and refused to let him in or give him any food.

Kokushi left the priest's house and many hours later he managed to reach the nearest village. The leader of the village told him he could stay there and he was given food and a place to sleep.

After eating he quickly fell asleep from exhaustion but only a couple of hours later he was woken by the villagers.

They told him that a man in the small village had just died and according to custom, the whole village were leaving their homes and going into the mountain to leave the corpse behind, alone, as part of the death rites that was their custom.

The exhausted traveller told the villager that he would stay where he was – he had been walking for hours without food or water and he was too exhausted to move, he said.

He added that he didn't believe in ghosts and spirits of the dead so he wasn't scared.

So that night he stayed alone with the corpse while all the villagers left.

Not long after, while he was trying to fall back to sleep, he thought he could see a shapeless dark figure.

He watched in terror as this figure came closer. In absolute horror he watched as it reached the corpse of the newly-dead villager and devoured the corpse, then departed silently.

When the villagers returned the next morning, he told them what he had seen, but they were not surprised to hear this.

As he was leaving, eager to get out of the area after the horror of the night before, he asked one of the villagers if the priest in the little house was conducting the funeral rites for this poor man whose body had been almost entirely consumed by the dark shape he had seen eating it the night before.

The villager told him that there was no priest nearby in a little house.

This baffled the Buddhist so he decided to go back to the little house and ask the priest why the villagers said he did not live there.

He went back to the place and found the same house there and the same priest, who had turned him away rudely the night before and refused to help him.

This time, the old priest immediately apologized for appearing rude the night before and then also apologized for appearing in his real form and eating the corpse in front of him.

He said that the shapeless dark and disfigured form he had seen eating the corpse had been him!

As you can imagine, Kokushi wanted nothing more than to run away as fast as his legs would take him but, the priest would not let him leave yet.

He sat him down and as Kokushi's entire body shook with fear, alone and miles from anywhere with this corpse-eating cannibal, the priest began to explain.

He explained that he had once been cursed and was reborn as a Jikininki because of the bad life he had led, full of greed and selfishness.

His punishment was that he had been cursed and doomed to this life he now had as part-priest-part corpse-eating Jikininki.

Jikininki still exist in Japan. They are said to be able to see in the dark, track a dying body, and do not die.

They are creatures of the night who roam the cemeteries but also the woods and the mountains, looking for any travellers who are lost and weakening.

They are waiting for them to die. They are even said to 'help' people to their deaths, by their ability to cause people accidents, such as car crashed, so that they will have a dead body to eat.

Watch out if you are ever alone at night in the middle of Japan, for you never know how close a Jikininki may be, just hoping to cause you a deadly accident so that it can feast on your dead body….

You're cordially invited to:

True Creepy Ghost Stories:

Hauntings, Ghosts,

Demons

and Monsters!

Come on in !!

Hector G. Grey

Chapter 3: Carew Castle

There are believed to be a few phantoms frequenting Carew Castle in Wales; a Celtic warrior is said to frequent the parapets and the apparition of a kitchen child may be the one who is causing the thumping of pots and skillets heard originating from the empty kitchen.

However, there's more! There is the tale of the 'white lady' who has been witnessed drifting from room to room and that of an ape too!

Many individuals from Carew town will let you know of their experiences with this 'white woman;' a wandering soul who strolls the vestiges in day-light or at the surge of the full moon. It is the apparition of Princess Nest, the most delightful lady in Wales, who still invites guests to her manor similarly as she would have done 900 years prior.

She was the girl of Rhys ap Tewder, the lord of Deheubarth, and she had spent some days at the court of King Henry I in London at the end of the 11th century. Henry went gaga for her and soon she brought forth his child.

It is said that to stay away from scandal inside his court, the married King organized that this young woman would be made to wed a Norman knight, Gerald de Windsor, Constable of Pembroke Castle.

She was not happy to hear that this was to be her fate, for she had never even met this man she was being ordered to marry. To try to make things up to her, the King said she could take her servant girl with her (who was a dear friend to her.)

Gerald de Windsor was actually a rather handsome man who was very much regarded by all who knew him. When he heard that he was to marry this young woman, though she was a beauty, he was still in mourning over the death of his most prized mistress. Notwithstanding, the marriage took place — Neither could disobey the King.

After getting married, they moved to Wales where the Castle was built, and, as the years passed they grew to love one another. Five more children were born.

She was still thought of as a great beauty and she still had many admirers, despite being a mother of 5. One of these admirers was her own cousin Owain. He was so smitten and obsessed with her that he even stormed the castle to kidnap her!

He took her away to his Castle and he got her pregnant twice before her husband could discover where she had been taken. He kidnapped her back — killing her cousin in the process. He died himself a few months later though.

And now, in mourning the Princess walks the castle grounds still searching for her dead husband, unable to let him go.

But now to the more curious ghost who roams the castle – the Barbary Ape!

 The story goes that Sir Rowland had one son who ran off with the daughter of a local   merchant - not a union that Sir Rowland approved of. Sir Rowland Rees, who lived at the Castle in the 18th Century, had once sailed around the Barbary Coast and during his trip he had rescued an Ape from a sinking galley ship. The Ape became his best friend! And he trained him to be able to respond to his every whim.

The story goes that his son, around this time, had run off with a local lass of lower social standing and this lass's father arrived at the Castle demanding to know what he was going to do to rectify the situation.

They got into a fight and it is believed Sir Rowland, on a night of a terrific storm and howling winds, let his Ape off its chain and the Ape attacked and killed the visitor. Before he died he cursed Sir for his evil action of allowing his Ape to attack him so violently and he swore he would have vengeance.

Legend has it that the ghost of this violent Ape returns to the Castle on dark stormy nights where he has been heard and seen by passers-by who hurry to leave the area fast.... before it can strike and tear them apart as it has done in the past.

Chapter 4: The Ancient Demon

The Ancient Ram Inn in Wotton-under-Edge, in Gloucestershire, England, is believed to have been witness to such chilling and evil events as black magic and child sacrifice, and it's believed to probably have more ghosts in residence than any other place in the whole of England, but then the Inn is also built on top of an ancient Pagan burial ground.

The Ancient Ram Inn possesses a sinister terrifying entity. It has been investigated by numerous international paranormal investigators ghost over the years but it rarely fails to terrify the most hardened of these investigators.

Many visitors and guests (it is a hotel too) have had the overwhelming feeling of being watched from the shadows and often these sensations are so strong that people have left, and refused to return.

The land upon which the old inn was built has shown evidence of burials and even human sacrifices! - Archaeologists found a grave with knives in it – and the body of a woman and child.

The room called 'the Bishops room' is believed to be where the most overwhelming paranormal events happen, with various spectral sightings in this room. The apparition of a young woman has been seen hanging from the ceiling. Visions of Monks have been seen on other occasions.

In the old horse stable which joins the Inn, unexplained tall dark shadows have been seen, making it nerve-racking for visitors who have been reported to become frozen to the spot with fear.

The Inn is ancient – it was built in 1145. There still remains parts of a tunnel system, which is thought to link the Inn with the local church, and it was once owed by a Priest.

A Bishop of Gloucester, the Right Reverend John Yates, once attempted to hold an exorcism to remove the malignant spirits but it didn't work. He told the local newspaper; "it is the most evil and abhorrent place I have ever had the setback to visit".

The Locals will openly tell you that they will cross over the street, rather than walk past the Ancient Inn at night-time.

Ker, one visitor says; "We went there tonight and we have seen orbs - I have photos that we took and we saw them. We have never been so scared in our lives - we have been inside and seen."

Chris Adams says; "I've been into the Inn and as I entered the bishops room it went stone cold and you could actually see your breath. I swear something gabbed my leg."

When the chimney in one of the bedrooms was opened up, black magic and satanic artefacts were discovered hidden inside. The two men who spent the night in that room were so disturbed that they had to go to a Priest to receive an exorcism.

The current owner, John Humphries, says that he has been dragged from his bed by violent entities – and raped, often, by the Inn's succubus. He says there are two demons resident and a witch, as well as unexplained strange glowing lights.

He says that when a local clergyman visited he said: 'I'm not going in there - what you've got in there is very, very evil.' He then adds; "Eight people who have spent the night here have had to be exorcised."

There are also many reports of a succubus that creeps silently into the beds of sleeping guests....

You're cordially invited to:

True Creepy Ghost Stories:

True tales of the restless;

Ghosts, Hauntings

Demons

and Monsters!

Come on in !!

ROGER P. HUNT

Chapter 18: Spook Road

Spook Hollow is the name for a road situated just outside of a small town in Missouri. The road dead-ends into a cemetery, which itself is creepy enough.

But, it is said that no matter what season you go there in, the weather inside the cemetery is always warm, then the lights start.

These spook-lights are mysterious as they dance their way across the gravestones. Where do they come from? What are they?

The area itself is located in between two towns and it is said that it has always been a place for witchcraft and satanic worship. Some who have gone to the graveyard have been chased out of it, by the sound of children screaming.

An old school bus sits along the road abandoned. Further down the road, a run down and dilapidated old house has dolls with broken limbs hanging from the trees beside it.

People have said that their cars have lost all power along that road and that their cars refused to start for at least fifteen minutes. They have been trapped there, alone in the pitch dark, too afraid to leave their car but stuck there, vulnerable to anything that might come....

Chapter 19: Haunted Hospitals

An anonymous nurse who worked in a hospital ward for care of elderly patients had been doing the same job for the last 15 years.

She had seen many things and experienced too much sadness, but what struck her most and what stayed in her memory the most was the night that started out like just any other night shift.

The patients would routinely be checked on every hour, and when the time came, the nurse began her first round and she noticed that a light was flashing in the doorway of room 312.

As she entered the room she saw nothing wrong. The patient was fine and relaxed in bed. And so, she left the room and continued checking on all the other patients' rooms.

Approximately an hour later, she began her round to check on the patients the second-time, and she's saw again that a light was flashing in the same room. But the patient herself was fine.

Well, it happened one more time and so she decided to take a closer look at the patient in room 312. When she went in the room, she found that the patient had the most terrified look on her face. She was staring at the corner of the room intensely.

Well the patient was elderly and she was also suffering from dementia, and so it wasn't perhaps that strange.

Unfortunately, the patient had also lost her ability to speak sometime before this, and so the nurse would not be able to ask her what was wrong anyway.

The patient was known to be a cheerful and gentle patient though. Although she was not well, she was still mobile, and the nurses were well used to hearing the sound of her shuffling feet as she made her way through her room and out into the hallways.

Not being a busy night and with no medical emergencies happening on the ward, the nurse decided that she would stay in the patient's room for a little while and sit in the chair next to her and perhaps this would bring her some comfort, because she was still staring intensely in the corner of the room at the ceiling.

Well only moments after the nurse sat down, sadly the patient very tragically passed away. A few hours after the patient had been taken care of, and prepared to be taken to the hospital mortuary, the nurse was putting the dirty laundry from her bed into a laundry basket, at the nurse's station, when she heard the very familiar sound of shuffling footsteps.

She looked up quickly, shaking her head. She turned to the other nurse at the nurses' station and said, did you hear that?

The nurse replied that she did hear. The shuffling sounds continued coming closer from down the hallway but then they seem to divert off into an area where some of the patients would go to watch television.

To this day the nurse who told this story is convinced that this was the ghost of the woman who had died only moments earlier that night, taking her last walk down the hallways where she had spent many months in the hospital, before she died.

Another anonymous nurse, an oncology nurse, who had been practicing again for at least 30 years, also describes her experience of witnessing something that you simply could not explain.

It has always stayed with her, always in her memory, as she has often thought of it but cannot explain it. It was when she was working the night shift, as she often did, at a state hospital.

On this particular night it had been very busy. There was one particular patient, a male patient who was very elderly and also in the final stages of cancer, and every time he would call for her, she would go to attend to his needs. And each time she left his room, no sooner had she gone, then he would start screaming out for her.

These were the chilling words that he said:
"Don't let it take me."

Finally, after the other patients had been taken care of, she heard him scream these words one more time. The nurse was freaked out after hearing this several times and it had given her goose-bumps and she had been so busy with all the other seriously ill patients, but now she finally had time to go and ask him what he meant.

She asked him who was going to take him, and the patient pointed toward the ceiling and said; "That black thing, up there!"

Only seconds later, the patient died in front of her....

If you like **<u>FREE BOOKS on Creepy True Ghost Stories</u>** –

come grab them here!!

Free books each & every week straight into your inbox!!

<u>www.mycreepybooks.com</u>

Want Some
FREE CREEPY BOOKS

Every Week???

- Yes, really! We send out FREE Creepy Books to our Subscribers every single Week!! – If you think that sounds pretty AWESOME, all you need to do is Sign Up!! – It's that easy!!

Subscribe here:

www.mycreepybooks.com

We love giving out CREEPY Books away FREE to our Loyal Readers - & all you have to do is keep an eye on your Inbox for all your FREE CREEPY Books ever single week!

www.mycreepybooks.com

p.s. if you enjoyed this book of chilling stories, please could you leave us a review on Amazon?

This helps us get these books in front of more people who love true ghost tales!!

Thank you so much, you are so awesome!!!!